R

by Murray Ogilvie

Lang**Syne**

PUBLISHING

WRITING *to* REMEMBER

LangSyne

PUBLISHING

WRITING *to* REMEMBER

79 Main Street, Newtongrange,
Midlothian EH22 4NA
Tel: 0131 344 0414   Fax: 0845 075 6085
E-mail: info@lang-syne.co.uk
www.langsyneshop.co.uk

Design by Dorothy Meikle
Printed by Ricoh Print Scotland
© Lang Syne Publishers Ltd 2014

ISBN 978-1-85217-289-3

Reid

*Echoes of a far distant past
can still be found in most names*

Chapter one:

Origins of Scottish surnames

by George Forbes

It all began with the Normans.

For it was they who introduced surnames into common usage more than a thousand years ago, initially based on the title of their estates, local villages and chateaux in France to distinguish and identify these landholdings, usually acquired at the point of a bloodstained sword.

Such grand descriptions also helped enhance the prestige of these arrogant warlords and generally glorify their lofty positions high above the humble serfs slaving away below in the pecking order who only had single names, often with Biblical connotations as in Pierre and Jacques.

The only descriptive distinctions among this peasantry concerned their occupations, like Pierre the swineherd or Jacques the ferryman.

The Normans themselves were originally Vikings (or Northmen) who raided, colonised and eventually settled down around the French coastline.

They had sailed up the Seine in their longboats in 900AD under their ferocious leader Rollo and ruled the roost in north east France before sailing over to conquer England, bringing their relatively new tradition of having surnames with them.

It took another hundred years for the Normans to percolate northwards and surnames did not begin to appear in Scotland until the thirteenth century.

These adventurous knights brought an aura of chivalry with them and it was said no damsel of any distinction would marry a man unless he had at least two names.

The family names included that of Scotland's great hero Robert De Brus and his compatriots were warriors from families like the De Morevils, De Umphravils, De Berkelais, De Quincis, De Viponts and De Vaux.

As the knights settled the boundaries of

their vast estates, they took territorial names, as in Hamilton, Moray, Crawford, Cunningham, Dunbar, Ross, Wemyss, Dundas, Galloway, Renfrew, Greenhill, Hazelwood, Sandylands and Church-hill.

Other names, though not with any obvious geographical or topographical features, nevertheless derived from ancient parishes like Douglas, Forbes, Dalyell and Guthrie.

Other surnames were coined in connection with occupations, castles or legendary deeds. Stuart originated in the word steward, a prestigious post which was an integral part of any large medieval household. The same applied to Cooks, Chamberlains, Constables and Porters.

Borders towns and forts – needed in areas like the Debateable Lands which were constantly fought over by feuding local families – had their own distinctive names; and it was often from them that the resident groups took their communal titles, as in the Grahams of Annandale, the Elliots and Armstrongs of the East Marches, the Scotts and Kerrs of Teviotdale and Eskdale.

Even physical attributes crept into surnames, as in Small, Little and More (the latter
being 'beg' in Gaelic), Long or Lang, Stark, Stout,
Strong or Strang and even Jolly.

Mieklejohns would have had the strength
of several men, while Littlejohn was named
after the legendary sidekick of Robin Hood.

Colours got into the act with Black, White,
Grey, Brown and Green (Red developed into Reid,
Ruddy or Ruddiman). Blue was rare and nobody
ever wanted to be associated with yellow.

Pompous worthies took the name
Wiseman, Goodman and Goodall.

Words intimating the sons of leading fig-
ures were soon affiliated into the language as in
Johnson, Adamson, Richardson and Thomson,
while the Norman equivalent of Fitz (from the
French-Latin 'filius' meaning 'son') cropped up
in Fitzmaurice and Fitzgerald.

The prefix 'Mac' was 'son of' in
Gaelic and clans often originated with occupa-
tions – as in MacNab being sons of the Abbot,
MacPherson and MacVicar being sons of the

minister and MacIntosh being sons of the chief.

The church's influence could be found in the names Kirk, Clerk, Clarke, Bishop, Friar and Monk. Proctor came from a church official, Singer and Sangster from choristers, Gilchrist and Gillies from Christ's servant, Mitchell, Gilmory and Gilmour from servants of St Michael and Mary, Malcolm from a servant of Columba and Gillespie from a bishop's servant.

The rudimentary medical profession was represented by Barber (a trade which also once included dentistry and surgery) as well as Leech or Leitch.

Businessmen produced Merchants, Mercers, Monypennies, Chapmans, Sellers and Scales, while down at the old village watermill the names that cropped up included Miller, Walker and Fuller.

Other self explanatory trades included Coopers, Brands, Barkers, Tanners, Skinners, Brewsters and Brewers, Tailors, Saddlers, Wrights, Cartwrights, Smiths, Harpers, Joiners, Sawyers, Masons and Plumbers.

Even the scenery was utilised as in Craig, Moor, Hill, Glen, Wood and Forrest.

Rank, whether high or low, took its place with Laird, Barron, Knight, Tennant, Farmer, Husband, Granger, Grieve, Shepherd, Shearer and Fletcher.

The hunt and the chase supplied Hunter, Falconer, Fowler, Fox, Forrester, Archer and Spearman.

The renowned medieval historian Froissart, who eulogised about the romantic deeds of chivalry (and who condemned Scotland as being a poverty stricken wasteland), once sniffily dismissed the peasantry of his native France as the jacquerie (or the jacques-without-names) but it was these same humble folk who ended up overthrowing the arrogant aristocracy.

In the olden days, only the blueblooded knights of antiquity were entitled to full, proper names, both Christian and surnames, but with the passing of time and a more egalitarian, less feudal atmosphere, more respectful and worthy titles spread throughout the populace as a whole.

Echoes of a far distant past can still be found in most names and they can be borne with pride in commemoration of past generations who fought and toiled in some capacity or other to make our nation what it now is, for good or ill.

Chapter two:

In the beginning

The origin of the Reid Clan is shrouded in mystery. Most Scots believe that the Reids are, along with the Duncans and Robertsons, descended from the Clan Donnachaidh, which is Gaelic for "Children of Duncan".

In Gaelic mythology all three clans are said to have originated with the same man. The clan's first chief was Stout Duncan who led his followers in support of Robert the Bruce at the Battle of Bannockburn, where he defeated King Edward II's army in June 1314. The next major chief was Duncan's great-grandson, Robert, who lived in the middle of the fifteenth century. His descendants called themselves Robert-son in his honour and this became Robertson. Not long after, a branch of the family, who were predominately red haired, called themselves Reid-Robertson. Reid is the Gaelic word for red. Through time the family dropped the Robertson part of the name and became known as Reid. Other Scottish families also took on the name, including MacRory (Mac Ruaraidh in Gaelic) who were from Islay. And those with the name Ruadh (meaning red) also changed to Reid. MacInroy became both Reid and Roy. In England and Scotland the names Reid, Reed, and Read signify "red" suggesting that the progenitor of the name had red hair or a ruddy complexion.

However, there is another school of thought that suggests the name may have originated much much earlier in Italy and arrived in Scotland via Bavaria.

At around 400 BC the Gauls over-ran central Italy, forcing the population to flee north. They settled in the Alpine region in what is now the Austrian Tyrol and part of Bavaria. They called themselves Rhedarians, which scholars believe is derived originally from Rhea, an ancient phoenician name. The capital of Phoenicia, Tyre, contained the districts of Ruad and Raad. The Rhedarians called their new home Rhaetia. The name survives to this day, in the

form of the Rhaetian Alps. The area was con-
quered by German tribes, known as Bavarians
and some of the Rhaedarian names were incorpo-
rated into the Bavarian language. For example,
the family name Reade was found in Bavaria. The
place name Reidlinggine, which means "the place
of the Reids" was also in Bavaria. Some of their
descendants are believed to have arrived in
Scotland during the Saxon invasion of Britain in
the fifth and sixth centuries and are thought to
have settled in the border region between
Nothumberland and south east Scotland. The
River Rede is found in this area and the valley
through which it flows is Redesdale. It was in this
area that many border battles between Scotland
and England took place. Consequently the bor-
derline between the two was constantly shifting.
This would account for Reids, Reades or Reeds
being found on both sides of the divide.

   While many well-known family members
are found in fourteenth century England, including those who lived south of the Border but
owned land in Scotland, the Scottish branch first

*Clan warfare produced a society where
courage and tenacity were greatly admired*

came to notice soon after the Battle of Flodden. In 1511 the French were under attack from the Holy League, a military alliance which included the Papal States, Spain, the Holy Roman Empire and England among others. They approached King James IV of Scotland in the hope of resurrecting the Auld Alliance. In return for supporting his crusades to the Holy Land and his claim on the English throne, he agreed. In September 1513 Scottish forces marched into England from Edinburgh and, having disposed of resistance just south of the border, encamped on Flodden Hill. Despite positional and numerical advantage the Scots, missing their most able gunners who had been despatched to the aid of the French, were annihilated. James and his son Alexander, who was the Bishop of St Andrews, died along with two abbots, 11 earls, 15 lords and at least 10,000 others. Among them was William Reade of Aikenhead, Clackmanan. His son, Robert, and the Reids who followed him had a major impact on life in Scotland and abroad.

Chapter three:

Important legacies

Robert Reid was born shortly before his father was killed in battle. The legacy he left when he died in 1558 is still benefiting the nation to this day.

Robert Reid followed a monastic life. He became Sub-Dean at Elgin Cathedral, then the abbot of the Cistercian monastery of Kinloss Abbey at Kinloss, Moray, where he increased the number of monks and built up the library. In 1528 he brought the Italian scholar, Giovanni Ferrerio of Piedmont to Kinloss. Ferrerio settled there and taught the young monks. Ferrerio's influence led to Kinloss becoming a centre of academic excellence. Robert Reid also held the priory of Beauly and was highly respected for his learning and wisdom. While abbot, he was sent on diplomatic missions as the king's commissioner, discussing peace with Henry VIII of England and going to France in connection with the marriage of James V of Scotland. In 1541 he became Bishop of Orkney. He continued as Commendator of Kinloss until 1553, then resigned in favour of his nephew, Walter Reid. From 1543 until his death he was Lord President (head) of the Court of Session, Scotland's supreme civil court. When he died he bequeathed money to set up a college in Edinburgh. This establishment is now better known as Edinburgh University.

James Reid was born in Kilmaurs, Ayrshire, in 1823 and served his engineering apprenticeship in Airdrie and in the Kilmarnock Foundry Company. In 1851 Reid went to work for Walter Neilson for the first time, as manager of the Hyde Park Street works in Finnieston, Glasgow. He left to go to Sharp, Stewart & Company of Manchester in 1858 but returned to manage Neilson's Springburn Works in 1863, later becoming a partner in the firm. James Reid eventually took over the firm and in 1893 his four sons became partners. In 1894 his son Hugh became senior partner. Four years later the company was renamed Neilson Reid and within two years it was the largest of its kind in Britain, employing 3,500 and producing 350 locomotives a year. Despite that success, in 1903 he helped to negotiate the amalgamation of Neilson Reid & Co with its major competitors, Sharp, Stewart & Co Ltd and Dubs & Co. The resulting limited company was known as the North British Locomotive Co Ltd. The first chairman of the company was William Lorimer, chief partner of Dubs & Co while Hugh Reid became deputy chairman and managing director with overall responsibility for the organisation and management. North British Locomotive Co Ltd was the biggest of its kind in Europe at the time, with 60 acres of works and nearly 8,000 employees. At its peak, production was averaging 447 completed locomotives per year. During the First World War in addition to locomotives the company produced shells, shell forgings, portable pill boxes, sea mines, planes, trench Howitzer carriages, tanks, military bridges, artificial limbs and machine tools. After the war competition began to bite and the orders for locos began to fall. But in the mid-1950s, it was still a world leader, employing

5,000 people. By 1963, exactly 100 years after James Reid took control it was all over and the company closed down. The Reids' legacy in that part of Glasgow remains to this day. The family built Belmont House, a sumptuous mansion. They donated the public halls, the land for Springburn Library and an extension to Springburn Park, the Winter Gardens and many other local amenities. Belmont House, which at the time sat on the city's highest point, was bequeathed on Hugh Reid's death in 1935 to Stobhill Hospital for use as a children's home in memory of his wife Marion who had died in 1913. It was later used as a nurses' living and training centre, before being demolished in 1986.

Samuel Chester Reid was the son of a Scottish Royal Navy officer. He was born in the USA and followed his father's footsteps into a career on the high seas. However, unlike his father, he joined the American navy and his heroic actions prevented a British victory in a decisive battle. He later went on to design the most enduring version of the Amercan flag, the Stars and Stripes.

Samuel was born in 1783. His father John, a lieutenant, was captured by the Americans in 1780 at a battle New London, Connecticut during the War of Independence. He was released on parole into the custody of Judge Chester in nearby Norwich and married his daughter Rebecca. Samuel joined the US navy as a boy and by the start of the War of 1812 was experienced enough to be made captain of his own privateer, *General Armstrong*. A privateer was a privately financed warship which had government approval to attack commercial shipping belonging to an enemy nation. The privateers were allowed to sell any goods they captured for profit. Unlike pirates, privateers were forced to cease their operations when peace was declared. In 1812, in response to a British blockade of American trade with France, the USA declared war on Britain. The British were fighting Napoleon and were angered by US trade support for the French. The British had also decided to punish the Americans by supporting the rights of American Indians against settlers. The *General Armstrong* left New York in

September 1814 and by the end of the month was
holed up in the Azores. Reid had 90 men under his
command and his small vessel was equipped with
seven guns. On September 26, as he sheltered in
the harbour at Fayal, the British attacked. Reid
should have been routed but he held out against
massively superior forces and firepower.
Eventually though, the British were able to board
the *General Armstrong* but in hand-to-hand fighting Reid and his men repelled the aggressors,
leaving them with huge losses, including the death
of the British commander at Reid's hands. That
night, under cover of darkness, Reid moved his
cannons from one side of his ship to the other and
waited for the British to attack again. At first light
the British struck again, with an 18-gun battleship.
But it was hit so many times by the Americans
that its crew was forced to abandon the battle and
limp away. By now the British had had enough
and sent the 74-gun *Plantagenet* to finish off the
American upstarts. But Reid had one more move
up his sleeve. As the *Plantagent* moved in for the
kill Reid scuttled his ship and he and his crew

headed to safety in the neutral harbour. The following day Captain Reid was invited to tea by British officers at the British consulate. Ignoring the fears of the American diplomats that it might be a trap he accepted and was warmly welcomed and feted as a brave and worthy foe. Reid's heroics were a remarkable achievement. But their true value wasn't immediately appreciated. By fighting such a brilliant rearguard action Reid delayed by ten days the arrival of the British fleet for the Battle of New Orleans. That extra time allowed the Americans to prepare their defences. The Battle of New Orleans took place on January 8, 1815 and was the final major battle of the War of 1812. American forces under General Andrew Jackson defeated a British army intent on seizing New Orleans, which was the gateway to the American west. After the war Reid became a war hero and was presented with many honors — including the thanks of Congress and the Medal of Honor, a gold sword from the State of New York and a silver tea service from the City of New York.

As a civilian Samuel Reid became harbour master for New York City, then as now one of the world's busiest ports. In 1818 the US flag was in need of a redesign. The original version was created to honour the first thirteen states, with thirteen stars and stripes. The second version contained fifteen stars and stripes to record the entry into the union of Vermont and Kentucky. But by 1818 there were 20 states and more were expected. Captain Reid proposed that the number of stripes should be fixed at thirteen and that the number of stars would represent the number of states. His idea was accepted by Congress and a new flag, whose design exists to this day, was born.

Chapter four:

Tragic Reids

John Reid, born in Bathgate in 1809, was the son of a well-to-do farmer and cattle merchant. There was no recognized school in his home village so he was dispatched to a local teacher whose specialist subject was Latin. Consequently, young John learned that language before he mastered English.

Despite that seeming setback he was brilliant enough to enter Edinburgh University at the tender age of 14. Initially he studied Latin, Greek and Maths, as it was his family's wish that he pursued a career in the church. However, he was attracted to medicine, particularly the study of anatomy and physiology. He'd already been a student for three years when he made the switch to medical school and it took another five years before he was able to graduate. In 1830 he finally left university qualified as a surgeon and physician. Dr Reid realised that he would require a great deal more knowledge and experience if he wanted to make a difference to society and a year later he moved to Paris, where he studied at the feet of several highly-distinguished physicians and surgeons. After 12 months of hard work and very little play in the French capital he was back in Scotland. Almost immediately he was asked to put his new skills into practice. Cholera had taken root in the country and was particularly widespread in the Dumfries area, where local doctors couldn't cope. Dr Reid was part of a four-man team of medics dispatched from Edinburgh to help control the outbreak. He had encountered the disease in Paris and was able to use his experience to combat it and bring it under control, which was achieved before it could spread through the rest of the country. Dr Reid's next mission was back in Edinburgh as a demonstrator, or tutor, in the School of Anatomy at Old Surgeons Hall. His job involved dissecting human remains in a bid to understand and explain to students the cause of death. Despite the ghoulish nature of his job he attacked it with vigour and enthusiasm, earning the respect of his contemporaries and gratitude of his students. Dr Reid subjected himself to a punishing schedule. He worked at the university from nine till four then, after a break, he began his private studies in the evening often continuing until the early hours of the next day. He apparently felt he worked at his best when the rest of the world was sleeping. Today he would be described as a workaholic. After three years his reputation was sky-high and he was appointed lecturer of physiology. Three years later, in 1838, he became the pathologist at Edinburgh Royal Infirmary. In 1839 Dr. Reid applied for the chair of medicine in King's College and the chair of anatomy in Marischal College, both in Aberdeen. He was unsuccessful both times, even though his pioneering work was now highly-regarded right across Europe. It wasn't long, though, before his abilities were recognized and in 1841 he assumed the prestigious professorship of anatomy at St Andrews University. Three years later he married Ann Blyth and for the next four years he happily turned his attention to the natural history of marine life in the area. He also published to great acclaim a collection of essays he'd written for scientific journals during his career. Everything was going well for Professor Reid and he was as happy as he'd ever been, surrounded by loving family and trusted friends. But suddenly, tragedy struck. He was in the prime of his life when a tiny blister appeared on his tongue. It grew into a bigger blister and was then diagnosed as cancer. The next 18 months were agonizing for him and his family as he slowly and painfully succumbed to the disease. He died on July 30 1849 aged just 40. His work was described by a contemporary thus: "As a physiologist he may be considered to have been unsurpassed. His volume contains more original matter and sound physiology than will be found in any work that has issued from the British press for many years."

James Reid From Angus became the first piper to be tried for high treason. He had served as a piper in the 1st Battalion, Lord Ogilvy's (Forfarshire) Regiment, raised in October 1745 in support of Bonnie Prince Charlie's rebellion and was among several men from this regiment left as part of the garrison of Carlisle when the Jacobites ended their invasion of England. In December that year James was captured by English forces when the city surrendered. At his trial he defended himself by claiming that as a piper he was a musician and not a soldier. He was not armed and therefore did not fight against the King. However the court decided that a Highland regiment never marched without a piper, and therefore his bagpipe, in the eyes of the law, is an instrument of war. The wording of the highly-controversial verdict was, "No regiment ever marched without musical instruments such as drums trumpets and the like; and that a Highland regiment never marched without a piper; and therefore his bagpipe, in the eyes of the law, was an instrument of war". The English jury recommended mercy but the judge ignored them and Reid was hanged, drawn, and quartered at York on November 15, 1746. This was seen by most people at the time and later as a judgment of revenge.

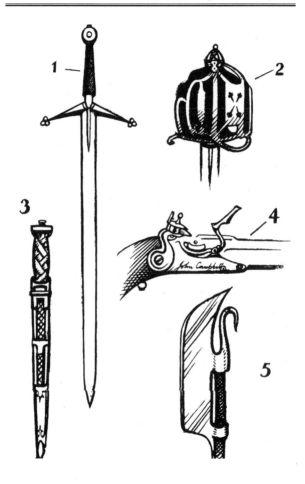

Highland weapons

1)   The claymore or two-handed sword
(fifteenth or early sixteenth century)

2)   Basket hilt of broadsword
made in Stirling, 1716

3)   Highland dirk
(eighteenth century)

4)   Steel pistol *(detail)* made in Doune

5)   Head of Lochaber Axe as carried
in the '45 and earlier